Sky High

PAIRED:

Two men with lofty goals. Barrington Irving (left)
loved to fly and refused to stop until he circled
the globe. Neil deGrasse Tyson became
obsessed with the stars and devoted
his life to learning about them.

"If you have a dream, you must put your energy toward making it happen. Don't let anyone tell you your dream isn't good enough."

Barrington Irving

"Beyond the judgment of others,

Rising high above the sky,

Lies the power of ambition."

from a poem by
Neil deGrasse Tyson

Photographs © 2012: Addictive Simulations/www.addictive.it: 29; age fotostock/Dirk
Renckhoff: 40; Alamy Images/James Nelis: 70; AP Images: 58 (Alan Diaz), 88 (Dana Edelson/
NBCU Photobank); Courtesy of Barrington Irving Sr.: 20; Corbis Images: 80 (Farrell Grehan), 78
(Roger Ressmeyer), 86 (George Steinmetz); Getty Images: cover (Diane Cook and Len Jenshel), 94
(Cate Gillon), 69 (Andrea Morini), 46 top (Marwan Naamani/AFP), 90, 91 (Dieter
Spannknebel), 67 (Ted Thai/Time & Life Pictures), back cover left, 3 left (Kevin Winter);
Jon Ross Photography/www.JonRossPhotography.com: 10, 14, 26, 32, 57; Courtesy of Juan
Rivera: 16, 37, 42, 43, 44, 49; MSNBC.com/David Friedman: 100; NASA: 99 (ESA/The Hubble
Heritage Team, STScI/AURA), 93 (J. Hester, A. Loll, ASU/ESA), 95 (JPL), 76
(JPL-Caltech), 12, 13 (NASA's Earth Observatory), 84 (SOHO/ESA & NASA), 96
(M. Weiss/CXC); NEWSCOM: 48 (bp1/Zuma Press), back cover right, 3 right
(k03/Zuma Press), 60 (Roger Smith/AURA/NOAO/NSF/AFP/Getty Images); Photo Researchers,
NY: 97 (Christian Darkin), 64 (Robin Scagell/SPL); ShutterStock, Inc.: 45 (H2O), 46
bottom, 47 (haider), 50 (jmatzick), 74, 75 (oorka); The Image Works/d Gamble/TopFoto: 62.

Library of Congress Cataloging-in-Publication Data

Stiefel, Chana, 1968-
Sky high / Chana Stiefel.
p. cm. -- (On the record)
Includes bibliographical references and index.
ISBN-13: 978-0-531-22558-5
ISBN-10: 0-531-22558-5
1. Irving, Barrington, 1983---Biography--Juvenile literature. 2. Air
pilots--United States--Biography--Juvenile literature. 3. African
American air pilots--Biography--Juvenile literature. 4. Tyson, Neil
deGrasse--Biography--Juvenile literature. 5. Astrophysicists--United
States--Biography--Juvenile literature. I. Title.
TL539.S765 2012
523.01092--dc22
[B]

2011008076

Tod Olson, Series Editor
Marie O'Neill, Creative Director
Curriculum Concepts International, Production

8 9 10   40   20 19 18 17

Sky High

Two men who couldn't keep
their feet on the ground

Chana Stiefel with Holly Peppe

Contents

TOUCH THE SKY: Barrington Irving

1 **Wild Ride**   14

2 **Charting a Course**   20

3 **Ticket to Fly**   26

4 **On the Runway**   32

5 **Globetrotting**   40

6 **Homeward Bound**   50

STAR POWER: Neil deGrasse Tyson

7 **The Kid on the Roof**   62

8 **Stellar Student**   70

9 **"Path of Most Resistance"**   80

10 **Star Quality**   86

A Conversation with the Author   102

What to Read Next   106

Glossary   108

Sources   110

Metric Conversions   110

Index   112

TOUCH THE SKY

Barrington Irving had come a long way for a
Jamaican immigrant from a tough section
of Miami. But to fly solo around the world,
at the age of 23? Even he had to wonder
whether he would make it home alive.

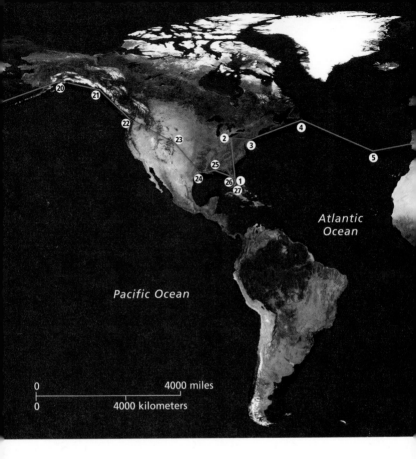

Circling the Globe

Barrington Irving became the youngest
person and the first black pilot to fly
solo around the world.

Indian Ocean

The Flight Path

1 Miami, Florida
2 Cleveland, Ohio
3 New York, NY
4 St. John's, Canada
5 Santa Maria, Azores
6 Madrid, Spain
7 Rome, Italy
8 Athens, Greece
9 Cairo, Egypt
10 Luxor, Egypt
11 Dubai, UAE
12 Mumbai, India
13 Kolkata, India
14 Bangkok, Thailand
15 Hong Kong, China
16 Taipei, Taiwan
17 Nagoya, Japan
18 Asahikawa, Japan
19 Shemya, Alaska
20 Anchorage, Alaska
21 Juneau, Alaska
22 Seattle, Washington
23 Denver, Colorado
24 Houston, Texas
25 Mobile, Alabama
26 Orlando, Florida
27 Miami, Florida

Barrington Irving was 23 years old when he began his solo flight around the world.

1
Wild Ride

Barrington Irving couldn't help glancing at the fuel gauge. When the needle hit the halfway mark, he knew there was no turning back. He had taken off from Canada in his single-engine plane, *Inspiration*. Now he had to reach the Azores, a chain of islands in the middle of the Atlantic Ocean. His plan, three years in the making, was underway. He was going to fly around the world— by himself.

Barrington Irving took this photograph as he flew across the Atlantic Ocean, a distance of nearly 1,600 miles.

Far below, he could make out the white-caps on the waves of the Atlantic. The view was beautiful, but Irving wasn't in the mood to appreciate it. He was all alone, climbing from 10,000 to 18,000 feet. If he had engine trouble, there was no place to land. He would have to ditch the plane in the ocean. And he couldn't swim. Not that he was likely to survive for long in the frigid water.

He wrestled his mind back to more positive thoughts. At 23, he was chasing his dream. If he succeeded, he would be the youngest person—and the first black pilot—to fly solo around the world. Thousands of young people were following his progress on his website. He wanted to show them that if they had a dream and determination, anything was possible.

Suddenly, a strange noise caught his attention. The loud whine of the propeller was changing pitch—higher, then lower, then higher again. "Don't panic," Irving told himself. "There's probably a simple explanation." When he calmed down, he realized it was just violently shifting winds rushing through the propeller blades.

Just when he was feeling comfortable again, the radio suddenly stopped picking up transmissions. Irving had been warned this might happen. Still, losing radio contact unnerved him. "Please acknowledge," he said into the microphone. He repeated the call over and over, his voice growing louder. "PLEASE ACKNOWLEDGE!"

Finally, the radio crackled back to life. Irving sighed with relief. Maybe he was going to make it after all.

Three hours later, the scattered islands of the Azores appeared on the horizon. He touched down and brought the plane to a stop. When he tried to get out, he found that his legs were stiff and weak. He had to stretch for 30 minutes before he was ready to climb out of the cockpit.

The truth hit him as he set his unsteady feet on solid ground. This nine-hour flight was only the first big test. There would be many more to come.

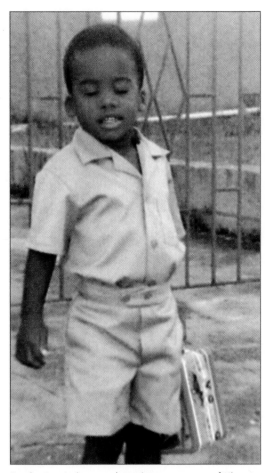

Barrington Irving was born in a poor area of Kingston, the capital of Jamaica. He and his family moved to Miami, Florida, when he was six.

2
Charting a Course

The Azores are an ocean away from Kingston, Jamaica, where Barrington Irving was born in 1983. Irving remembers his years there fondly. There were coconut trees and cool ocean breezes.

There were also plenty of things for a curious mind to explore. Barrington spent hours in a garage watching his uncle fix cars. He pestered his mother with questions: "How does the washing machine work?" "How many people did it take to build our house?" "How do birds fly?"

But while Barrington explored, his parents made plans for the future. Seeking a better education for their children, they moved the family to Miami, Florida. Barrington was six at the time. His brother Ricardo was three.

Miami was a shock to Barrington. Drugs and violent crime plagued their new neighborhood. Gunshots and police sirens were familiar sounds. "My parents really sheltered us," Irving remembers. "We weren't allowed to leave our yard."

Barrington struggled to adapt to his new life. As the new kid in town, he felt left out. School bullies targeted him. They made fun of his Jamaican accent. They cracked jokes because he didn't wear nice clothes or name-brand sneakers. "Someday, I'm going to do something great," he told himself, "something that will make the other kids wish they'd given me a chance."

At Miami Northwestern High School, Barrington faced more serious challenges. Classmates were taking drugs and dropping out of school. Fights broke out in the halls. Many kids were headed for jail—or worse. One boy was caught by the police in the middle of a robbery and shot seven times in the chest.

Barrington began to lose hope for the future. "As a kid, I never thought I would live past my twenty-fifth birthday," he says.

During Barrington's freshman year, a friend urged him to try out for the football team. The Miami Northwestern Bulls had been ranked as high as third in the entire nation.

If Barrington made the team and played well, he could end up with a college scholarship. He might even get a shot at the National Football League. "It might give you a ticket out of the hood," the friend said.

In 1997, Barrington made the team as a 5'8", 197-pound freshman. He became a rising star, starting out at center and later moving to fullback. Wearing the black, blue, and gold uniform gave him a new feeling of confidence. Girls noticed him. Even the neighborhood thugs started to show some respect.

For once, Barrington's future was looking up. He had made a name for himself in his high school. He had a new little brother named Christopher. And his father had opened a Christian bookstore, which the entire family helped to run.

One day, Barrington was working in the bookstore when a Jamaican man walked in wearing a dark blue uniform. Barrington's eyes widened. "I had never seen a black pilot before," he recalls.

The man introduced himself as Captain Gary Robinson. He and Barrington talked for a while. Then, out of the blue, Robinson posed a question: "Have you ever thought of becoming a pilot?"

"No way," Barrington replied. "I don't think I'm smart enough. Don't you have to be a genius to be a pilot?"

Robinson laughed and shook his head. "You have to have a passion for what you do," he said.

It was the beginning of a friendship that would change Barrington Irving's life.

Irving's mentor was Captain Gary Robinson (right), a pilot for United Airlines. Robinson said of the teenage Irving, "There was something in his eyes that told me he wanted to do it. He just didn't know he could."

The day after Captain Robinson walked into the Irving family bookstore, he drove Barrington to the airport. He gave the 15-year-old a tour of a Boeing 777 passenger jet.

Barrington was fascinated by the huge aircraft. In the cockpit, there were dozens of buttons, dials, and gauges. He made Robinson explain the purpose of each one.

Sitting in the captain's chair, Irving could imagine himself flying a plane. "Man!" he said. "If only I could learn to fly!"

"You can do whatever you want if you want it badly enough," Robinson replied.

Barrington went home that day knowing exactly what he wanted. He went to the library and borrowed every book and video about airplanes he could find. He signed up for free trial subscriptions to flight magazines. To earn money for flying lessons, he cleaned swimming pools and bagged groceries at a supermarket. Lessons started at $110 a session. But while he saved, he found a cheaper alternative. He bought flight-simulation software for $40 and installed it on the bookstore computer. While he was working, he began teaching himself to fly.

When Barrington's senior year arrived, his new passion faced its first real test. Several colleges offered him football scholarships.

Irving bought flight-simulation software to learn about flying. This software re-creates the experience of landing in thousands of real-life airports.

It was the goal he and his teammates had been working toward for the past four years. Barrington turned down all the offers.

His coaches and teammates thought he was crazy. How could he walk away from an opportunity to play for the best universities?

But within a year of his graduation, Barrington's decision paid off. He won a full scholarship to study aviation and the science of flight at Florida Memorial University (FMU). The scholarship covered college costs *and* flight lessons.

At FMU, a historically black university, Irving studied and polished his flying skills. He was busier than ever. But something Captain Robinson had said stuck with him: "I helped you. Make sure you help someone else."

Irving decided to volunteer at schools in low-income neighborhoods. He spoke to students about his passion for aviation. He encouraged them to walk away from crime, drugs, and violence.

But the more he talked, the more he realized that talking wasn't enough. He needed to *do* something, and it had to be inspiring. Then the idea hit him: What if he flew solo around the world?

Irving told Captain Robinson about his idea. Robinson said he would be happy to help Irving raise the money to buy plane tickets. Then Irving clarified that *he* would be the pilot, circling the globe on his own.

"You'd be the *pilot?!*" Robinson exclaimed.

Irving couldn't stop smiling.

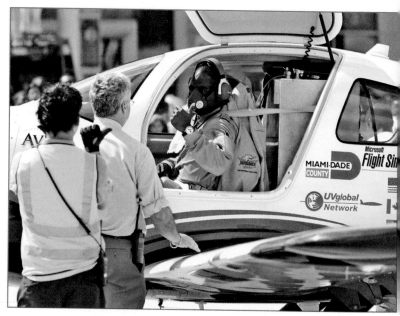

Irving signals that he has completed the preflight check of his plane. Pilots must verify the status of their planes' fuel gauges, wing flaps, rudders, and more before they can take off.

4
On the Runway

Before he could fly around the world, Irving needed a plane. But who would donate an expensive aircraft to an unknown 21-year-old?

Irving decided that if he couldn't get a whole plane, maybe he could convince different companies to donate the parts. He went after the most crucial part first—the engine.

In the fall of 2005, Irving drove 12 hours from Miami to Mobile, Alabama. He parked near the headquarters of Continental Motors and slept in his car to save money. The next morning he dressed in a suit and tie and asked to meet with the president of the company, Brian Lewis.

Irving had never talked to Lewis and didn't have an appointment. But after a two-hour wait, Irving was ushered into the president's office. "You've got five minutes. Shoot!" Lewis said.

Irving spilled out his life story. Then he outlined his mission: to fly solo around the world. Finally, he asked Lewis to donate an engine.

"Thank you, Mr. Irving," was Lewis's only response.

Driving home, Irving had no idea whether he had convinced Lewis to help. But a few weeks later, he got a phone call from Lewis's office. The engine was his!

Once other companies learned that Irving had been given an $83,000 engine, they jumped on board. Before long, Irving had collected $300,000 worth of parts. And a manufacturing company in Oregon, Columbia Aircraft, agreed to assemble the plane.

Irving had just been promised a single-engine plane that could take him around the world. The plane would be ready in March 2007, and he set his takeoff date for that month.

In the meantime, Irving had a lot to do. He had to plan his route and master the flight skills he would need. He practiced flying in all kinds of weather. He flew cross-country. He flew over mountains.

He made long flights over the ocean—from Miami to Jamaica and on to South America. The long flights helped him get used to the cramped conditions in a small cockpit.

He invited his friend and old football buddy, Juan Rivera, to join him on a number of his practice flights. Rivera, a film student, began shooting footage of Irving for a documentary about the around-the-world adventure.

To plan his route, Irving contacted Keith Foreman at Universal Weather and Aviation in Houston, Texas. Foreman's team of flight planners and weather experts designed a route for Irving's journey. The route would take Irving to 27 cities in six weeks.

During his practice flights, Irving wore a flight suit like the one on the left. He also practiced water rescues, using an inflatable life vest (right) and an inflatable raft. This training was terrifying because Irving didn't know how to swim.

As his takeoff date neared, Irving worried about the dangers that lay ahead. The small plane carried barely enough fuel to get through the longest flights. If bad weather struck, he might not have the fuel to detour around it.

Cold temperatures posed another hazard. His tiny plane wouldn't have the de-icing equipment that large jetliners had. If ice formed on the wings, it could disrupt the airflow and knock Irving out of the sky.

There were so many unknowns. Irving had to ask himself: Was he really ready to fly 30,000 miles around the world—alone?

On March 23, 2007, he set his doubts aside, at least for a few hours. More than 3,000 schoolkids and other supporters gathered at Miami's Opa-Locka Airport for Irving's send-off. Everyone cheered as he addressed the crowd. "If you have a dream, you must put your energy toward making it happen," he said. "Don't let anyone tell you your dream isn't good enough."

When Irving finished speaking, his parents and Captain Robinson escorted him onto the runway. They prayed together and hugged. Finally, Irving climbed into the cockpit of his brand-new plane, *Inspiration*.

This was it. This was the moment he had been working toward for nearly four years. He taxied across the airfield, opened the throttle, and sped down the runway. *Inspiration* lifted off and soared toward the horizon.

For the first major stage of Irving's journey, he flew 1,600 miles, from St. John's, Canada, to the Azores Islands. This is Santa Maria Island, where he landed.

Two weeks later, Irving had survived his first big test, the 1,600-mile flight across the North Atlantic Ocean. He landed safely in Portugal's Azores, a string of islands 1,000 miles west of the mainland.

He had more confidence than ever. The ordeal over the North Atlantic had boosted his morale. He had never flown that long in a single stretch. It was the first test of all his planning and training. He felt like a load had been lifted from his shoulders.

Europe: Italy and Greece

On April 9, 2007, Irving left the Azores for Europe. His friend Juan Rivera joined him in Madrid, Spain. Rivera would be following

The Forum in Rome

Irving to capture the journey on film.

Irving and Rivera spent ten days touring Europe. "I had never been overseas before," Irving recalled. "I was amazed by the graceful architecture and the centuries of history hiding in the streets."

After Madrid, the two met up in Rome, Italy. Irving and Rivera visited the Forum, the ruins of a public square in ancient Rome. They discussed what life might have been like before automobiles and airplanes.

They toured the Roman Colosseum, where gladiators once battled lions and alligators. Irving threw a coin in the Trevi fountain. According to legend, that guaranteed that he would return to Rome someday.

Throwing a coin into the Trevi fountain in Rome

From Rome, Irving and Rivera went on to Athens, Greece. They saw the Parthenon, a famous Greek temple. They also visited an ancient stadium.

The Parthenon in Athens

Irving had a demanding schedule that was a real struggle to keep up with.

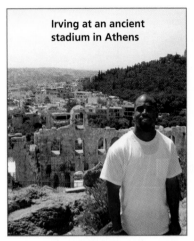

Irving at an ancient stadium in Athens

Every time he landed in a new city, he would talk to fans and reporters at the airport. At each stop he had to arrange for the ground crews to refuel and repair his plane.

Even after he checked into his hotel there was more to do. He wrote blog posts to keep fans updated. He studied weather forecasts and news about his route. And he always tried to find the time to go exploring with Rivera.

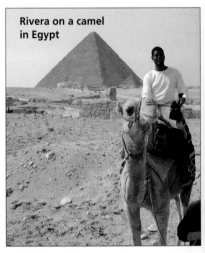

Rivera on a camel in Egypt

Minarets in Cairo

Middle East: Cairo, Egypt

After Athens, the next stop was Cairo, Egypt. But sandstorms in the Egyptian desert grounded Irving for three days.

On April 19, he was able to take off. The following day, he found himself riding a horse in front of the ancient pyramids outside Cairo. "Man!" he said to Rivera, who was perched on a camel. "Can you believe we made it this far?"

An indoor ski resort in Dubai

Middle East: Dubai, United Arab Emirates

On April 22, Irving touched down in Dubai in the United Arab Emirates. Dubai is one of the wealthiest cities in the world.

"I stayed in a hotel that looked like a palace, went four-wheeling in the desert, and visited a ski resort located inside a mall," Irving said.

The Dubai skyline

In Dubai, flight mechanics noticed that *Inspiration* had serious problems. Dust and sand from the desert had clogged the brake lines. A battery needed replacing.

Irving was grounded, and the delays put him in real danger. Every summer, monsoon storms bring heavy rain and strong winds to the countries around the Indian Ocean. Irving had hoped to pass through the region before the storms hit. Now that seemed impossible.

Asia: India and Thailand

On May 10, Irving landed in Kolkata, India. The monsoon season was in full swing, and it was a week before he could take off. He made it to Bangkok, Thailand, and collapsed in his hotel. But the weather was closing in fast. He still had to cover more than 1,000 miles to make it to Hong Kong. By early the next morning, he was airborne again.

Monsoon season in Kolkata

Asia: Hong Kong, China

In the skies over Vietnam, a fierce monsoon storm engulfed *Inspiration*. Irving wrestled with the steer-  ing yoke as winds pounded the tiny plane. A downward current of air drove *Inspiration* toward the earth.

Irving on a street in Hong Kong

Irving dropped 10,000 feet in seconds. Another current pushed him upward just as suddenly. Irving prayed the winds would not flip the plane or hurl it into the mountains.

After fighting through the most terrifying hours of his life, Irving touched down safely in Hong Kong. He found his hotel and fell into a deep sleep.

The Aleutian Islands, off the coast of Alaska, are often blanketed with fog. Irving was headed for Shemya, a tiny island near the tip of the Aleutian chain.

6
Homeward Bound

By the end of May, Irving had arrived in northern Japan. Once again he found himself stranded by the weather. Cold, dreary rain with whipping winds and thick clouds kept him grounded for two weeks. He was trapped in a tiny hotel room in the town of Nakashibetsu, with nothing but rice fields for miles around.

Irving was lonely and homesick. His around-the-world quest was supposed to take six weeks. Now it had stretched to ten. He worried that people would forget what he was trying to accomplish.

Meanwhile, he still had the toughest leg of the trip ahead of him—across the North Pacific Ocean to Shemya, Alaska. Irving was dreading the flight. When he tried to sleep, he had flashbacks to his trip across the Atlantic. He had been rested and strong for that flight. Since then he had lost 30 pounds. He was worried he would be too weak to handle the next leg of the trip.

The crossing to Shemya presented major challenges. It was a 1,700-mile, ten-hour flight with nowhere to land in an emergency. Shemya was a tiny island in the Aleutian island chain. Dense fog blanketed the area from June through September. If he failed to land in Shemya, he probably wouldn't have enough fuel to reach another airfield.

On June 9, the skies over Nakashibetsu cleared. The weather opened up between two storms over the North Pacific. Irving knew this was his best chance to make the crossing. He called his family and flight team to say good-bye, trying his best to sound confident.

The Pacific crossing proved to be every bit as hard as he'd expected. Wind gusts blew from every direction, making *Inspiration* shake and roll. Irving clutched the controls, eyeing the waves below. "If I need to ditch the aircraft, would anyone ever find me?" he wondered.

Hour after hour of rough flying wore him out. Then, about an hour out of Shemya, Irving watched a wall of monstrous clouds rise in front of him. The storms inside would be ferocious.

Irving made a snap decision to climb above the clouds. He put on his oxygen mask so he could breathe at the higher altitude, but the air tank soon ran out. As he cleared the cloudbank, he started feeling light-headed and weak.

He braced himself for the descent. On the way down through the dense cloud cover, Irving noticed ice forming on his wings. "We are ten minutes from landing! Hold on!" he yelled at *Inspiration*. He gritted his teeth and sped down. He came out on the other side above one of the most beautiful sights he had ever seen—the Shemya runway.

Irving guided *Inspiration* to a stop. He was completely exhausted and could barely muster a smile for the people who had come out to greet him. But he and his plane were back on U.S. soil.

In the weeks that followed, Irving completed the American circuit of his world tour. He stopped in Anchorage, and then Juneau, Alaska; Seattle, Washington; Denver, Colorado; then Houston, Texas; Mobile, Alabama; and Orlando, Florida. He made speeches at each stop and felt like a rock star as fans greeted him and asked for his autograph.

On June 27, 2007, Irving made his final approach to Miami's Opa-Locka Airport. Thousands of supporters were waiting to welcome him back. As he lined up his approach, Irving waggled *Inspiration's* wings in a traditional pilot's greeting.

After landing, the homesick pilot climbed down from the wing of his plane. He embraced his family, Captain Robinson, and others who had helped his dream get off the ground.

Barrington Irving, the curious kid from a tough neighborhood in Miami, had made history.

With his feet back on the ground, Irving devoted himself to his main mission— inspiring kids to follow in his footsteps. His nonprofit organization, Experience Aviation, runs summer camps and after-school programs where students can learn about flying. "Believe in yourself," Irving likes to tell his students. "Believe that you are talented and powerful and important and can make a difference in the world."

In the summer of 2008, Irving helped 60 students build a plane from a kit. When it was fully assembled, he climbed into the cockpit and flew into the sky.

After Irving's around-the-world journey, he mentored young people who built this plane—*Inspiration 2*. Here, Irving has just successfully completed the plane's first flight.

At the end of his historic flight, Irving was greeted at
Opa-Locka Airport by his family. Shown left to right
are Barrington's brothers, Ricardo and Christopher;
his father, Barrington Sr.; and his mother, Clovalyn.

Barrington Irving

Born:

November 11, 1983

Grew up:

Kingston, Jamaica, and Miami, Florida

Life's work:

Mentoring young people and promoting careers
in aviation and related fields

Website:

www.experienceaviation.org

Favorite books:

*The E-Myth Revisited: Why Most Small Businesses
Don't Work and What to Do About It,*
Michael E. Gerber
The 48 Laws of Power, Robert Green
Robinson Crusoe, Daniel DeFoe
Private Pilot Manual, Jeppesen Sanderson
Twenty Thousand Leagues Under the Sea,
Jules Verne

Author of:

*Touch the Sky: My Amazing Solo Flight Around
the World,* with Holly Peppe

He says:

"It's important to remember that the toughest
times in your life can be useful later on because
they teach you patience and make you realize
how strong you really are."

STAR POWER

As a kid, Neil deGrasse Tyson was the biggest geek around. And he didn't care who knew it. Now he's a successful astrophysicist—and one of the most famous geeks in the galaxy.

Neil deGrasse Tyson has been fascinated by astronomy since he was a child. He is now one of the most famous astrophysicists in the world.

7
The Kid on the Roof

Neil deGrasse Tyson grew up in New York City wanting desperately to become an expert in the planets, stars, and outer space. He might as well have been a skier growing up in the desert. The city was a terrible place for stargazing. Clouds and smog usually masked the night sky. Even on clear nights, the city lights drowned out the faint twinkle of the stars.

That wasn't enough to discourage Neil. When he was 14, he saved about $100 by walking people's dogs. With some help

A 50-mm refracting telescope, the type often used by amateur astronomers, is focused on the constellation Orion.

from his parents, it was enough to buy a five-foot-long telescope. Night after night, he carried his new treasure to the roof of his apartment building. Appropriately enough, the 20-story building was named Skyview Apartments.

Sometimes Neil turned his little sister into his assistant. Between the two of them, they hauled the telescope and a 100-foot extension cord up the stairs. The telescope had an electric device that tracked specific stars as the earth turned. But the roof had no power outlets. So Neil lowered the cord over the edge. A family friend who lived on the nineteenth floor pulled the cord through the window and plugged it in.

Through the telescope, Neil had the night sky in his grasp. He could see stars, planets, and the moon in eye-popping detail. And that—more than anything else—made him happy. For Neil deGrasse Tyson, a clear night seen through a telescope was heaven on earth.

Neil was nine when he discovered what he loved most. It came to him during a field trip to New York City's Hayden Planetarium. For 45 minutes he sat in the planetarium and stared at the domed screen. Images of planets, stars, galaxies, and meteors danced overhead. Neil was in love—with the sky.

By sixth grade, he had discovered the name for a scientist who spends his life studying the universe. From then on, he answered "astrophysicist" when someone asked what he wanted to be when he grew up. "The study of the universe would be my career," he later wrote, "and no force on Earth would stop me."

Children watch a show in the Hayden Planetarium in 1978.
The planetarium was later rebuilt. It reopened in 2000.

Not even the New York Police Department.

During one of Neil's nighttime visits to the roof, people in neighboring buildings grew suspicious. The telescope looked like a grenade launcher. The extension cord could have been a rope lowered by a burglar. At the very least, the figure on the roof might have been spying on people through their windows.

Before long, police arrived to check out the complaints. According to Tyson, he soon had them peering through his telescope, identifying stars and planets. That wasn't the last time police officers interrupted Neil's stargazing. But they always left with an appreciation for the wonders of the universe. "For all I know," Tyson recalls, "I would have been shot to death on numerous occasions were it not for the majesty of the night sky."

This photo of the New York City skyline was taken from a rooftop in the 1970s. That's when Neil deGrasse Tyson was on his own rooftop, gazing up at the stars. His view was obscured by light pollution—the artificial light that shines upward into the sky.

This photograph of the moon's south pole was taken using a telescope that can magnify images by up to 250 times. Tyson's "grenade launcher" telescope could magnify images by up to 300 times.

8

Stellar Student

Astrophysics wasn't the most obvious career choice for Neil deGrasse Tyson. There was his urban upbringing, for one. For another, there was the color of his skin. Tyson is African American, and when he was a kid, the number of black astrophysicists could be counted on one hand.

There was also his performance in school. During his elementary years, teachers complained that he talked too much and didn't focus on his work. "Neil should cultivate a more serious attitude toward his schoolwork," his third-grade teacher wrote on his report card. In fifth grade, his teacher noted, "[Neil] is somewhat lax about completing his work, compositions, notebook, etc. He needs to be encouraged and prodded."

But Neil had something that isn't always taught in the classroom: curiosity. He loved to explore the world around him and figure out how it worked.

One night, when Neil was 11, a friend shared a pair of binoculars with him. He told Neil to point them above the buildings and check out the stars. Neil focused in on the moon. "It wasn't just pretty," Tyson recalled. "It was another world, with mountains, valleys, craters, and hills . . . I was hooked."

In sixth grade, Neil finally found a teacher who recognized his love of astronomy. She urged him to take after-school courses at the Hayden Planetarium. The classes were intended for older kids and adults, but she was sure that Neil could handle the material.

Neil won people over with his single-minded passion. His parents, Cyril deGrasse Tyson and Sunchita Feliciano Tyson, had never studied astronomy. But they couldn't resist their son's enthusiasm. For Neil's twelfth birthday, they bought him his first small telescope.

Soon they were combing bookstores for bargain science books. They ferried Neil to libraries and special classes. They drove him to parks where the stars could be seen

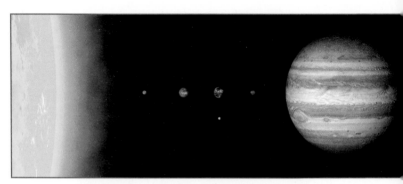

This diagram of the solar system shows the relative sizes of the planets. The distances between them are not to scale. The sun is at the far left. Then, from left

more clearly. "We used New York City as a learning lab," his mother said.

To Neil, stargazing was much more than a hobby. He learned how to observe and take notes on sunspots—dark blots on the sun's surface. He measured the rate of the sun's rotation. He studied Venus, Jupiter, and Jupiter's moons. And he fell in love with Saturn. In seventh-grade shop class, he built a lamp modeled after the ringed planet. His

to right, the planets are Mercury, Venus, Earth, Mars, Jupiter, Saturn, Uranus, and Neptune. The dwarf planet Pluto is at the far right.

mother drove him to half a dozen hardware stores to find the supplies.

Neil's dedication led him to some exotic experiences. At 14, he won a scholarship to observe a solar eclipse—from a ship off the northwest coast of Africa. As he and the other passengers watched, the moon moved between the sun and Earth, completely blocking the sun. Tyson also got to spend a summer in the California desert at a camp for space-obsessed kids.

This diagram shows Jupiter and its four largest moons. Io has many active volcanoes. Scientists think Europa may have twice as much water as Earth. Ganymede is the largest moon in the solar system. The surface of Callisto is four billion years old.

Back in New York, Neil enrolled in the Bronx High School of Science, a place he calls "Nerd Central." It was the kind of school where students study through lunch and jump at the chance to do projects for extra credit.

He did have other interests besides his telescope. At 6´2″ and 190 pounds, he played basketball and was the captain of the wrestling team. "I was a nerd who could kick your butt," he says.

But he was a nerd nonetheless—and he didn't mind. He didn't worry about fitting in. As long as he had his telescope and his books, he was happy.

When it came time to apply to colleges, Tyson knew exactly what he wanted. He had read science magazines to find out

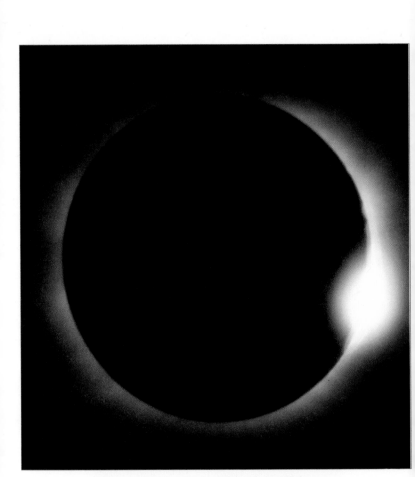

Tyson witnessed this solar eclipse from off the coast of Africa when he was 14. This is called a diamond ring image. The moon is completely blocking the sun—except for a ring of light around the moon's perimeter and a bright burst of light to the side.

where the best and brightest astrophysicists taught. Harvard University was ranked at the top, so Neil was determined to study there.

Not everyone shared Neil's vision for his life. His guidance counselor thought he should attend a school with a good wrestling program. "She could only see me in the stereotypical role of black male athlete," Tyson recalled.

Neil ignored her and applied to five schools, including Harvard. The following year, he was on his way to Cambridge, Massachusetts. He was now a student at Harvard University, Class of 1980.

Rowers race on the Charles River, which flows alongside the Harvard University campus. Tyson joined the crew team his freshman year.

9

"Path of Most Resistance"

Entering Harvard as a freshman, Tyson walked under an ivy-covered arch. On it was inscribed, "Enter to Grow in Wisdom." He took the message to heart. He majored in physics—the science of matter, energy, motion, and force. But he also studied literature, music, and art. He rounded out college life by rowing crew and earning a spot on the wrestling team.

One day after wrestling practice, a team-mate asked him what he was studying.

When Tyson told him he was majoring in astrophysics, his friend looked surprised. He suggested that Tyson do something more helpful to black communities.

Tyson was stunned. Astrophysics had been his passion since he was a boy. But was he being selfish in some way? How would studying the stars help anyone?

Tyson put his doubts aside and stuck with his career path. He graduated from Harvard and went on to the University of Texas at Austin. There he earned a master's degree in astronomy and met his future wife, Alice Young. He then returned to New York City to pursue his doctorate in astrophysics at Columbia University. While he studied, he traveled to space observatories around the world. He researched the shape of the Milky Way galaxy and investigated other cosmic mysteries. He published papers about his work.

He was still at Columbia when he got a phone call from a TV news station. The station wanted an expert opinion about explosions on the sun's surface. Tyson went to the studio and taped a two-minute interview. He reassured viewers that the blasts posed no threat to Earth.

Tyson raced home to watch the broadcast. Seeing himself on TV felt like an "out-of-body experience," he says. But something else hit home. Here he was, a black scientist, sharing his knowledge with the world. He realized the influence he could have on young people, especially black kids. "For the first time . . . I stood without guilt for following my cosmic dreams," he says.

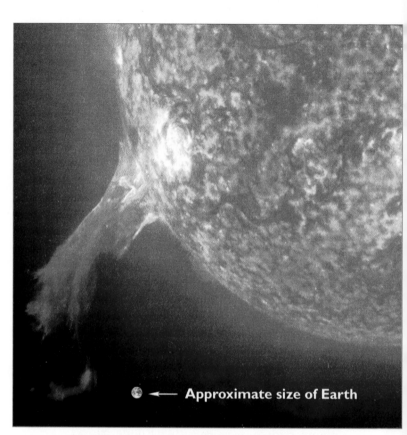

← Approximate size of Earth

This photo of a solar flare was taken by SOHO, a European spacecraft. Solar flares are huge explosions that erupt from the sun's atmosphere into space.

In May 1991, he received his PhD from Columbia. Dr. Neil deGrasse Tyson was one of only seven black astrophysicists in the entire country.

Tyson was asked to address his class of PhD candidates at graduation. He spoke about the goal he had been pursuing for more than half his life. "There were few parts of society that were prepared to accept my dreams," he told the audience. "I wanted to do with my life what people of my skin color were not supposed to do. As an athlete, I did not violate society's expectations. To be an astrophysicist, however, became a 'path of most resistance.'"

Tyson had found his path when he was nine years old. Following it had opened up a new universe to him.

The Hayden Planetarium is shown against the New York City skyline. A theater inside the sphere shows simulations of the birth of the universe, the deaths of stars, and other cosmic fireworks.

10
Star Quality

Tyson's star continued to rise. After earning his PhD, he taught and did research at Princeton University in New Jersey. Then, in 1994, he was asked to return to the Hayden Planetarium. In 1995, he was named the planetarium's director. He was no longer some wide-eyed kid. He was the man in charge.

In that role, he has become one of the highest-profile scientists in the country. News organizations have taken notice. He is smart and distinguished. He has a great

Tyson appeared on *Late Night with Jimmy Fallon*
with Orlando Magic star Dwight Howard and British
billionaire Richard Branson. Branson is the founder
of Virgin Galactic, which is planning to offer space
travel to private citizens.

sense of humor and a talent for explaining complicated science in a simple way. When a space-related issue makes the news, reporters call him first for an interview.

Tyson uses his popularity to raise scientific awareness. He writes books and publishes articles in popular magazines. He serves on government commissions to study the space program. He gives lectures at planetariums and other sites around the country.

When Tyson speaks about astronomy, he is funny and relaxed. He looks like he's having fun. And why not? He spends his days thinking and talking about the issues that have captured his imagination since childhood.

Neil deGrasse Tyson writes and lectures on a variety of topics related to astrophysics. What follows are a few of his favorites.

If an asteroid with a diameter of few miles struck Earth, it would release as much energy as several million nuclear bombs.

Asteroid Collision

Look out! According to Tyson, a giant asteroid called Apophis may be on a collision course with Earth.

Apophis is about the size of a football stadium. Some scientists say it could plunge into the Pacific Ocean in 2036. If

it does, it would cause unimaginable damage. "The tsunami it creates will wipe out the entire West Coast of North America, bury Hawaii, and devastate all land masses on the Pacific Rim," Tyson says.

Most scientists, including Tyson, think Apophis will likely miss Earth. But there's good reason to think that an asteroid will eventually hit home. After all, it's happened in the past. It's believed that the dinosaurs—and almost all other life on Earth—were killed off by a massive asteroid strike 65 million years ago.

Should we figure out ways to deflect killer asteroids away from our home planet? Tyson thinks so—unless we want to end up like the dinosaurs.

Seeds of Life

Can you imagine the explosion of a star that's 50 times the size of the sun? A supernova occurs when a massive star no longer has the fuel to resist the strong, inward pull of its gravity. The core of the star begins to collapse, heating up to a temperature of 100 billion degrees! All that energy makes the star explode into space. It is the most impressive firework show in the universe.

Tyson says that these "spectacular deaths" are actually necessary for life. Supernovas create elements like carbon, iron, and oxygen. When they explode, they share these materials with the rest of the galaxy. So our planets—and even our bodies—are partially made of exploded stars!

The Crab Nebula is the result of a supernova that was observed in 1054.

Where Did Life Begin?

Were our ancestors Martians? In 2004, Tyson hosted a TV series called *Origins*. He took viewers on a journey back to the beginnings of the universe, Earth, and life itself. In one of the episodes, Tyson suggested that long before there was life on Earth, asteroid collisions may have blasted

A Martian meteorite that landed on Earth in 1911

chunks of rocks from Mars into space: "Bacteria, stowed away in the nooks and crannies . . . could have traveled to Earth . . ." he said in the show. Some of those bacteria just might have been the source of life on Earth. "It may be that we're all descendants of Martians," he said.

Why Space Travel?

It's a sizzling 860° F on Venus. The surface of Mars used to have water, but now it's bone-dry.

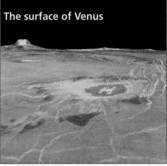

The surface of Venus

Something *bad* happened on these planets, Tyson says. It's our job to discover what it was, so that Earth doesn't become a barren wasteland too.

This is why Tyson pushes for a new generation of space travel. He wants NASA to send people back to the moon. He wants to see robots dispatched to Mars and beyond. People need to care about what happens on other planets, he insists. The more we know about outer space, the easier it will be to protect the future of life on Earth.

Death by Black Hole

What would happen if you fell feet first into a black hole, a dark region in space where the pull of gravity is so high that even light is too slow to escape?

According to Tyson, the gory scene would unfold like this: Your feet would be sucked

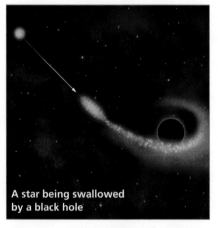

A star being swallowed by a black hole

into the black hole faster than your head. The difference between the force pulling on your feet and the force pulling on your head would stretch your body like a rubber band. At the same time, you'd be squashed "like toothpaste squeezed through a tube," Tyson says. His term for this process: "Spaghettification."

Do Aliens Exist?

In the past few years, scientists have discovered hundreds of planets orbiting stars other than our sun. Could one or more of those planets harbor life?

Aliens are unlikely to look human.

Not necessarily, Tyson says. He points out that many of these planets are gas giants like Jupiter. They have no solid surface where life as we know it could live.

On the flip side, he says, "Compelling arguments suggest we are not alone." The ongoing discoveries of new planets show that Earth is not unique. "To declare that Earth must be the only planet with life in the universe would be inexcusably bigheaded of us," Tyson says.

The Next Tyson

Who is going to figure out how to protect Earth from killer asteroids? Who will find signs of life in space or the secret to Mars's past? The next great astrophysicist could easily be a nine-year-old who, like Tyson, was inspired by a visit to a planetarium.

That's the kid who Tyson wants to reach with his work. He wants to make sure science is cool and understandable. He wants to share his passion for the sky with a new generation of kids.

"What you need, above all else," he says, "is a love for your subject, whatever it is. You've got to be so deeply in love with your subject that when balls are thrown, when hurdles are put in place, you've got the energy to overcome them."

This galaxy, M82, is 12 million light-years away. It is five times as bright as our galaxy. This photo was taken by the Hubble, an orbiting telescope that captures what Tyson calls "spectacular images of the cosmos."

Neil deGrasse Tyson stands in front of models of Saturn
and Jupiter at the Hayden Planetarium.

Neil deGrasse Tyson

Born:
October 5, 1958

Grew up:
The Bronx, New York City

Life's work:
Studying the universe and promoting
science education

Day job:
Astrophysicist and Frederick P. Rose Director of the
Hayden Planetarium

Website:
www.haydenplanetarium.org/tyson

Author of:
Death by Black Hole: And Other Cosmic Quandaries
Just Visiting This Planet
The Pluto Files: The Rise and Fall of America's
    Favorite Planet
The Sky Is Not the Limit: Adventures of an
    Urban Astrophysicist

He says:
"There are no limits when you are surrounded by
people who believe in you, or by people whose
expectations are not set by the short-sighted attitudes
of society, or by people who help to open doors of
opportunity, not close them."

A Conversation with Author
Chana Stiefel

Q *How did you go about researching this book?*

A I had a manuscript that Barrington Irving and his manager and publicist, Holly Peppe, wrote about his round-the-world trip. I also consulted Irving's web site, and I interviewed him twice over the phone.

Unfortunately, Neil deGrasse Tyson wasn't available for an interview. Luckily, he has published a memoir called *The Sky Is Not the Limit*. I also read books he wrote about space. Dozens of articles in magazines and even a few online video clips helped me get a better picture of Tyson's character. And the Hayden Planetarium website was filled with interesting info.

Q *These profiles are both about the subjects' journeys to define themselves. What do you think are their defining characteristics?*

A Both Irving and Tyson have drive, nerve, and passion. Maybe most important, they're both very resilient. They don't take no for an answer, and they bounce back when they hit obstacles. Tyson, for instance, refused to listen to the guidance counselor who tried to discourage him from applying to Harvard. When Irving was trying to build his plane, a lot of people refused to donate parts. He just pressed ahead until he got the president of Continental Motors to give him an airplane engine.

Both Irving and Tyson also have a good sense of humor, which comes in handy when they hit bumps in the road. And they have a knack for surrounding themselves with positive and supportive people.

Q *Irving and Tyson were athletes. Has their experience with sports had an impact on their careers?*

A Athletes need to be disciplined to stick to a routine and keep their eyes on the prize. For Tyson, being a wrestler gave him tenacity (or determination), which helped him reach his academic goals. For Irving, being a football player gave him strength to endure the physical hardships of flying solo.

Q *You're a science journalist. Why do you like writing about science?*

A When I was a kid, I thought science was really dull. But I realized there is science in *everything* we do, whether we're eating, sleeping, playing sports, listening to music, or texting.

A Conversation with
Holly Peppe

Peppe is Irving's manager and publicist. She wrote a detailed account of his journey that became the main source for the profile "Touch the Sky."

Q *How did you meet Barrington Irving?*

A I met Barrington in 2006, when he was planning his trip around the world. He wanted to show other young people that if he could achieve his dream, they could too. He asked me for assistance because I had experience with the international media. I had been public relations director for a medical organization that travels to developing countries to do eye surgery out of a jet specially equipped as a hospital.

Q *As Irving's manager and publicist, what kind of work do you do for him?*

A I help Barrington make decisions that will further his career. I also work closely with the companies that sponsor his visits to schools nationwide. During his round-the-world trip, I coordinated communications between him and his support team.

In my role as publicist for the flight, I wrote press releases and text for his website. I also set up appearances for him on CNN, the NBC Today Show, and other media outlets. His story was featured in thousands of articles, on more than 400 radio shows, and in 900 TV segments that reached more than two million people.

Q *What was the greatest challenge for you?*

A Those of us on Barrington's support team felt like we were traveling around the world with him. Because his journey took him through many of the times zones in the world, it was often necessary to stay up through the night to follow his progress.

Q *Please describe your writing process.*

A I was always jotting down notes from my conversations with Barrington about the flight. I also interviewed the people closest to him—his parents and brothers, Captain Robinson, and his best friend Juan Rivera.

During the flight, Barrington wrote journal entries that he sent to me every few days to post on his website. I edited those entries and included them in the book. I also included comments from the many students, teachers, pilots, and others who sent Barrington messages, cheering him on.

What to Read Next

Fiction

Black Holes and Uncle Albert, Russell Stannard. (160 pages) *A girl and her uncle travel to places where time and space do not behave normally.*

Cosmicomics, Italo Calvino. (153 pages) *This is a book of whimsical stories about the evolution of the universe.*

Flygirl, Sherri L. Smith. (288 pages) *A black teenager pretends she's white so that she can fly during World War II.*

George's Secret Key to the Universe, Lucy and Stephen Hawking. (336 pages) *A world-famous scientist and his daughter have written an adventure story based on space science.*

Icarus at the Edge of Time, Brian Green. (34 pages) *Physicist Brian Green re-imagines the myth of Icarus, transporting it to the cosmos.*

The Martian Chronicles, Ray Bradbury. (288 pages) *Stories about the colonization of Mars by Earthlings.*

Nonfiction

Black Eagles: African Americans in Aviation, Jim Haskins (208 pages) *African American achievements in aviation.*

Fly the Hot Ones, Steven Lindblom. (128 pages) *What it's like to take off, fly, and land eight different planes.*

The Sky Is Not the Limit, Neil deGrasse Tyson. (204 pages) *Tyson tells his life story in this memoir.*

Touch the Sky: My Amazing Solo Flight Around the World, Barrington Irving and Holly Peppe. (112 pages) *Irving describes his record-breaking flight.*

Universe, edited by Martin Rees. (512 pages) *This book is packed with information, photographs, and illustrations.*

Books

Twentieth-Century Space and Astronomy: A History of Notable Research and Discovery, Marianne J. Dyson. (272 pages) *During the twentieth century, people's understanding of Earth and its place in the universe progressed by leaps and bounds.*

Airplane Flying Handbook, edited by the Federal Aviation Administration. (288 pages) *This book is the official government guide to piloting aircraft—a must-have for anyone who wants to learn how to fly.*

The Airplane: How Ideas Gave Us Wings, Jay Spenser. (352 pages) *The author explains every aspect of the development and evolution of airplanes.*

Films and Videos

Journey to the Edge of the Universe (2009). *This National Geographic DVD takes the viewer on an amazing voyage from Earth to the edge of the universe.*

The Magic of Flight (1996). *This DVD explains what makes planes fly and shows amazing stunts performed by the U.S. Navy's Blue Angels.*

One Six Right: The Romance of Flying (2005). *This documentary tells the history of one small airport in California.*

Websites

www.nasa.gov
NASA's site includes news, information, and space-related videos.

www.haydenplanetarium.org
The Hayden Planetarium's site presents news, photographs and videos about space.

www.experienceaviation.org
This is Barrington Irving's site, and it includes a lot of information about his historic around-the-world flight.

Glossary

air traffic control (AIR TRAF-ik kuhn-TROHL) *noun* the management of aircraft in the air and on the ground. An air traffic controller's primary mission is to prevent planes from colliding.

asteroid (ASS-tuh-roid) *noun* a rocky object in outer space that is much smaller than a planet

astronomy (uh-STRON-uh-mee) *noun* the study of stars, planets, and outer space

astrophysicist (ass-troh-FIZ-uh-sist) *noun* a scientist who studies the physical properties of outer space

bacteria (bak-TIHR-ee-uh) *noun* microscopic life-forms

black hole (BLAK HOHL) *noun* a region of space where gravity is so strong that even light cannot escape. Black holes are formed when a star's core collapses during a supernova.

doctorate (DOK-tuh-rate) *noun* the highest academic degree awarded by a university

force (FORSS) *noun* an action that changes the shape or the movement of an object

galaxy (GAL-uhk-see) *noun* a system of ten million to 100 trillion stars that is bound together by gravity

master's degree (MASS-turz DIG-ree) *noun* a degree awarded by a university to students who complete at least one year of specialized study after graduating from a four-year college

matter (MAT-ur) *noun* anything that has weight and takes up space as a solid, liquid, plasma, or gas

mentor (MEN-tor) *noun* a trusted teacher or guide

meteor (MEE-tee-ur) *noun* a streak of light in the sky made by a small space object burning up as it enters Earth's atmosphere

monsoon (mon-SOON) *noun* a seasonal shift in the wind patterns of a region

NASA (NASS-uh) *noun* the National Aeronautics and Space Administration; a U.S. government organization responsible for space exploration and research

PhD (PEE AYCH DEE) *noun* doctor of philosophy; a person who has a doctorate degree

planetarium (plan-uh-TAIR-ee-uhm) *noun* a theater for reproducing the positions of the sun, moon, planets, and stars onto a curved ceiling

restricted airspace (ri-STRIKT-id AIR-spayss) *noun* part of the airspace controlled by a local authority that pilots cannot fly through without permission

solar eclipse (SOH-lur i-KLIPS) *noun* when the moon comes between the sun and the earth, blocking some or all of the sun's light

sunspots (SUHN-spotz) *noun* dark spots that appear at times on the sun's surface

taxi (TAK-see) *verb* to drive a plane along the ground before taking off or after landing

tsunami (tsoo-NAH-mee) *noun* a very large, destructive wave caused by an asteroid strike or an underwater earthquake or volcano

Sources

TOUCH THE SKY

Author's interview with Barrington Irving in 2010.

Interviews with Barrington Irving by Holly Peppe.

"At 23, the Youngest Pilot to Solo the Planet," Vincent M. Mallozzi. *New York Times*, July 18, 2007.

"Back Talk with Barrington Irving," Sheiresa McRae. *Black Enterprise*, September 1, 2007.

"Barrington Irving Making History." *National Weekly*.

Barrington Irving's speech at Opa-Locka Airport. Miami, Florida, March 23, 2007. (including quote on page 4)

"Cessna 150 Preflight," Ken Shuck. Cessna150.net.

"Experience Aviation," Barrington Irving. ExperienceAviation.org.

"Our Boy," Ingrid Brown. *Jamaica Observer*, August 4, 2007.

"Pilot Shares Story of Success," Laurie D. Willis. *Salisbury Post*, November 6, 2010.

"Sweet Inspiration: Passing the Baton," Frances Fiorino. *Business Aviation Now*, April 17, 2007. (including quote on page 26)

Touch the Sky: My Amazing Solo Flight Around the World, Barrington Irving and Holly Peppe. New York: Scholastic, 2012.

"Trailblazing Black Pilot Inspires Students at Astoria School," Nathan Duke. *New York Post*, January 20, 2010.

"Young Pilot Flies with 'Inspiration,'" Gordon Williams. *Jamaica Gleaner*, March 26, 2007.

Metric Conversions
feet to meters: 1 ft is about 0.3 m
miles to kilometers: 1 mi is about 1.6 km
pounds to kilograms: 1 lb is about 0.45 kg
degrees Fahrenheit (F°) to degrees Celsius (C°) formula: $\dfrac{5 \times (F° - 32)}{9} = C°$

STAR POWER

"Astrophysicist & Tie Collector: Neil deGrasse Tyson." Nova Science video podcast via mefeedia.com. (including quote on page 93)

"A Conversation with Neil deGrasse Tyson," Peter Tyson. NOVA, June 29, 2004. (including quote on page 96)

"The Dark Side," David Owen. *New Yorker*, August 20, 2007.

Death by Black Hole: And Other Cosmic Quandaries, Neil deGrasse Tyson. New York: W. W. Norton & Company, 2007. (including quotes on pages 94, 98, 99)

"A Guide to Buying Your First Telescope," Don Urban. Rockland Astronomy Club, 2010.

"Jupiter: Moons." NASA.com.

"Looking Up: Astrophysicist Neil deGrasse Tyson," Jimmie L. Briggs. *Crisis*, May–June 2006. (including quote on page 85)

"More than a Science Show," Alex Strachan. *Gazette*, September 27, 2004.

"Neil deGrasse Tyson Walks the Dog," Tom Miller. PBS.org, April 23, 2010.

The Sky Is Not the Limit, Neil deGrasse Tyson. Amherst, NY: Prometheus Books, 2004. (including quotes on pages 5, 66, 68, 71–72, 83, 85, 99)

"Star Power: As an Astrophysicist, Neil deGrasse Tyson Is a Universal Expert," David Segal. *Washington Post*, December 16, 2007. (including quote on page 74)

"Super Stargazer: Astrophysicist Neil deGrasse Tyson," Charles Whitaker. *Ebony*, August 2000. (including quotes on pages 72, 79)

"The Time 100: Neil deGrasse Tyson," Michael D. Lemonick. *Time*, May 3, 2007. (including quote on page 77)

The Universal Book of Astronomy: From the Andromeda Galaxy to the Zone of Avoidance, David Darling. Hoboken, NJ: Wiley & Sons, 2004.

Index

Aleutian Islands, Alaska, 50, 52

aliens, 99

asteroids, **90–91**, 90–92

Athens, Greece, **43**, 43, **44**

Azores, 15, **40**, 41

black holes, 98, **98**

Cairo, Egypt, **45**, 45

Columbia University, 82–83

Continental Motors, 34–35

Dubai, United Arab Emirates, **46**, 46–47, **47**

flight simulator, 28, **29**

flight suit, 37

Florida Memorial University, 30

Foreman, Keith, 36

galaxy, 97

Harvard University, 79, **80**, 81–82

Hayden Planetarium, 66, **67**, 73, **86**, 87

Hong Kong, China, 48–49, **49**

Inspiration, 10, 14, 26, **32**, 33–35, 39

Irving, Barrington, 3, 14, 20, 26, 32, 37, 43, 44, 49, 58
  childhood, 21–23
  in high school, 23–24, 28, 30
  global route, **12–13**, 36
  starts solo flight, **32**, 39
  completes solo flight, 55, **58**

Japan, 51

Jupiter, 74

Kolkata, India, **48**, 48

life vest, 37

Madrid, Spain, 42

Mars, 94–95

meteorite, 94

monsoon, 47, **48**, 48–49

moon, the, 70

moons of Jupiter, 74, **76**

Princeton University, 87

Rivera, Juan, 36, 42–45, **44**

Robinson, Captain Gary, 25, **26**, 27–28, 31, 39, 55

Rome, Italy, **42**, 42–43, **43**

Shemya, 52–54

solar eclipse, 75, **78**

solar flare, 84

solar system, **74–75**

supernova, 92–93, **93**

Tyson, Neil deGrasse, 3, 62, 88, 100
  childhood, 63, 65–66, 68
  at school, 71–73, 77
  doctorate, 82, 85

University of Texas, 82

Venus, 74, 95, **95**